Sonnets from the Portuguese

Silhouette of Elizabeth Barrett Browning,
done in Florence seven years after her
marriage to Robert Browning.

ELIZABETH BARRETT BROWNING

Sonnets from the Portuguese

ILLUMINATED BY THE
BROWNINGS' LOVE LETTERS

EDITED BY
JULIA MARKUS &
WILLIAM S. PETERSON

THE ECCO PRESS

THE ECCO PRESS
100 West Broad Street
Hopewell, New Jersey 08525

Published simultaneously in Canada by
Penguin Books Canada Ltd., Ontario
Printed in the United States of America

Library of Congress Cataloging-in-Publication Data

Browning, Elizabeth Barrett, 1806–1861.
    Sonnets from the Portuguese : illuminated by the Brownings'
love letters / edited by Julia Markus & William S. Peterson.
        p.   cm.
    ISBN 0-88001-451-2 (alk. paper)
    1. Love poetry, English. 2. Browning, Elizabeth Barrett,
1806–1861—Correspondence. 3. Women poets, English—19th
century—Correspondence. 4. Sonnets, English. 5. Love-letters.
I. Markus, Julia. II. Peterson, William S. III. Title.
PR4189.A1 1996
821'.8—dc20   95-43253

Designed and typeset by William S. Peterson
The text of this book is set in Monotype Centaur
and Monotype Columbus

9 8 7 6 5 4 3 2 1
First Edition

Contents

Illustrations

'And Love Is Fire'

A New Look at *Sonnets from the Portuguese*

BY JULIA MARKUS

OW DO I LOVE THEE? Let me count the ways." Everyone recognizes that line from Elizabeth Barrett Browning's *Sonnets from the Portuguese*. Yet who today can quote another line from her sequence of forty-four love poems? Printed and reprinted, often in a small format suggesting quaintness rather than strength, the *Sonnets* stand as proof that when we take something for granted, we can easily cease knowing it at all. It is time to take a fresh look at these remarkable poems. They contain the deepest and at times the darkest thoughts of a woman of genius, in grave health, who finds in middle life not the death she waits for but the love she never expected.

In the hundred and fifty years that have passed since Elizabeth Barrett wrote the *Sonnets from the Portuguese* in secret, in the bedsitting room of her father's house at 50 Wimpole Street, where she had lived as a confirmed invalid, there has been no attempt to connect them visually and concretely to the love letters she was writing to Robert Browning at the same time. Robert was the younger poet who suddenly and miraculously entered her life in January 1845 and seems to have fallen immediately in love with her. She was used to admirers exaggerating their feelings for her in letters. She would never have dreamed that this new year would also offer her a new life. For the next twenty months before she and Robert married secretly and left London for Italy, they wrote 574 letters to each other; all but one, in which he impulsively told her of his love after their first meeting, survive. Although the link between the letters and the sonnets has often been alluded to, the imagery of her sonnets has generally been compared to Shakespeare's and the Italian form of her sonnet sequence to Petrarch's. There has been no concentration on the fact that it was her "life in a new rhythm" that she was celebrating and that the idiom of the sequence is inspired mainly by her own experience of awakened love, often in the imagery of the love letters.

The purpose of this volume is to present the *Sonnets* in an entirely new context. The large size of the page allows the sonnets the stature they deserve. Each poem is printed on the right-hand page and is accompanied on the left with excerpts from the love letters. The verbal echoes – at times sad, witty, erotic – between the poems and the lovers' letters will be apparent and will allow readers to glean for themselves the living context out of which these poems arose. Where else in our literature can a sequence of poems by a major writer be so intimately and movingly connected to the lived life that inspired them?

The selections from the letters we have chosen (and certainly we chose from an embarrassment of riches) not only point to the striking verbal similarities between letter and sonnet but also allow the reader to follow the secret courtship of the Brownings from its beginning up through the day, three years after their marriage, when Elizabeth showed Robert the sonnets for the first time. It has to be remembered that Elizabeth Barrett never thought of publishing these sonnets. They – just like the couple's mutual attraction and courtship – were a result of love and passion, not of poetic ambition and literary device. When Robert convinced Elizabeth to publish them, they were tucked into her volume of poems of 1850 in approximately the sequence in which they were written and disguised through an obscure title. Sonnet 42 (once Sonnet 17 in manuscript) was not published with them, and there might have been some shuffling before the sequence in the early, incomplete version at the Pierpont Morgan Library was established. Still, in general the poems seem to have been kept, like their love letters, as a reminder of the spontaneous progression of their love.

And Love Is Fire

When Robert Browning saw that Elizabeth Barrett had praised his po-etry in a poem of her own in 1844, he did not write to thank her. At 32 years old, six years Elizabeth's junior and far less famous than she, he did not wish to be seen as one of those people who rush in on the "Medicean Venus" in order to "cut their initials" in her. He had in fact just returned from Italy, where such graffiti could be seen on ideal statuary, and he planned to return there as soon as possible. He was an intense and hand-some young man who did not believe in romantic love and had dedicated his life to writing out his soul in poetry. It was Elizabeth's cousin and his friend, John Kenyon, often mentioned in the letters, who urged Robert to write to Elizabeth, as he was certain Elizabeth would enjoy hearing from him.

Enjoyment did not come easily to Kenyon's frail but youthful-looking cousin. She had been a child prodigy, spending her earliest days in her fa-ther's elaborate mansion in a remote part of England. The oldest of twelve children of Mary Graham-Clarke and Edward Barrett Moulton Barrett, she was used to wealth, natural beauty, and isolation. The first of the Barretts to be born in England — not Jamaica — in over two hundred years, she experienced first hand what it was like to be the descendent of a fabulously wealthy colonial planter family who had made their money in Jamaica on the backs of slaves. Her father was never really at home in England, and when lawsuits and the slow ending of slavery reduced his means, the family moved finally to London, where he could oversee his daily business concerns. Elizabeth's mother, who had nurtured her tal-ents, died when the poet was 22, a tired woman who had bent under the temper and strong will of her husband. Elizabeth, who had been healthy and adventurous in youth, never fully recovered from an illness she had at the age of 14 and was often an invalid, having severe, if misdiagnosed, problems with her lungs. She was given to asthmatic attacks and bouts of hemorrhaging. From the age of 14 she was treated with morphine, which, to the end of her life, she believed to be the medicine that kept her alive.

She was a dutiful and loving daughter of Edward Barrett Moulton

Barrett but at the same time quite conscious of what she called the area of his peculiarity. She aided her younger siblings in snatching the innocent pleasures they could, in the usual way, behind his back. For Moulton Barrett, a Nonconformist (in the English religious sense), believed that the father of the family should be obeyed as completely and zealously as the Father in heaven. And he would not permit his children to socialize with those of the opposite sex outside of the family, for he would not allow any of his children, male or female, to marry.

When Robert finally wrote to Elizabeth Barrett on January 10, 1845 (excerpted on page 1 of this edition), he had no idea of the conditions Elizabeth lived under at 50 Wimpole Street. She was by then 38 years old, a world-famous poet, wondered and whispered about by her loyal fans in England and America. They knew her through her words, and many would have gone to lengths to see the invalid recluse in person. What they did not know was that by 1845 Elizabeth Barrett was suffering with not only bodily but also psychic ills. For in 1840 her heart had been broken, and with it went her spirit, and to a large extent her will to live.

By then she had lost her mother whom she adored, as well as her grandmother and her uncle Samuel, both of whom had left their brilliant and charming grandchild and niece money of her own. She had also just lost her brother Sam, who had been sent back to Jamaica to oversee the estates now that slavery was abolished. Elizabeth was intensely opposed to slavery and to her father's sending his siblings back to Jamaica. In fact, Edward Barrett Moulton Barrett had wanted to send his oldest son and namesake, Elizabeth's favorite brother, "Bro," back to Jamaica. Her mother excepted, there was no one Elizabeth was closer to than this brother, who was only sixteen months her junior and with whom she had shared childhood and tutors until he was sent, at 13, to school. The profligate Sam went to the Barrett estates in Jamaica in Bro's place, while Bro brought Elizabeth to the sea at Torquay for her health. Then, at Elizabeth's encouragement, he stayed on, though their father was displeased. Elizabeth was also trying to help Bro financially, perhaps because he wanted to get married. But whatever the family circumstances, as will be evident in the letter facing Sonnet 5, Bro went out sailing on a calm day at Torquay with two other accomplished sailors, never to return. Elizabeth's grief and guilt concerning her drowned brother, whose body was washed to shore months after, tugged her downward to the grave. She lost every semblance of self-esteem. Although, with her usual bravery, she did not show her grief after the initial torment and went on with her poetry, she buried herself in her bedsitting room at Wimpole Street, waiting to die. Five years later she received a letter from Robert Browning instead. The next night she wrote excitedly to a friend that she had just received word from "Browning the poet . . . king of the mystics." In her first sonnet, originally entitled "Death or Love" she relates that a "mystic Shape" moved

> *Behind me, and drew me backward by the hair;*
> *And a voice said in mastery while I strove, . .*
> *'Guess now who holds thee?' — 'Death!' I said, But there*
> *The silver answer rang . . 'Not Death, but Love.'*

Death or Love was the choice Elizabeth Barrett faced in 1845. After more than four months of correspondence with Robert, she allowed him to visit while her father was at work. As the correspondence and the weekly visits continued, Elizabeth gained strength. Her doctor, who was also physician to Queen Victoria, felt that she would not survive another winter in London and advised that she go to Italy for the winter of 1845–46. By then, Robert had made it clear that he would do no more traveling without her, and the couple had thoughts of meeting in Pisa, where she would be for her health. Her father was totally against this trip, although he had no idea of her romantic involvement. It was then that Elizabeth realized that Moulton Barrett did not love her as much as she had thought, and that he literally would prefer her death to her leaving Wimpole Street. Robert's comments on this are found opposite Sonnet 12, and in Sonnet 16, realizing fully his devotion, Elizabeth ends her "strife." By late September 1845, she decides that if Robert invites her forth, she will rise to his love. That is, *if* she should live.

And Love Is Fire

Her inner conflict, displayed throughout the sonnet sequence, was not about obeying or disobeying her father. She believed as a mature Christian woman she had not only the right but the responsibility to make her own decision whether or not to marry. Although her siblings were financially dependent on her father's whims, she, through her inheritances, even had enough money to act (Sonnet 24). Only in one sonnet (35) does she express ambivalence about leaving home. Her deepest inner conflict was whether grief could be transformed by love, the past supplanted by the present, whether Robert could redeem her from her grief and guilt over Bro.

In Sonnet 5 she is as clear as the poem is powerful. If, like Electra, she pours out the ashes of her grief over her brother's death at Robert's feet and he stamps them out, fine and good. But if some of those ashes do not go "to darkness utterly," if the wind stirs them to life, the fire could not only burn up all of Robert's poetic ambition but scorch him bodily as well. So searing is the death of Bro, so powerful is her own strain of morbidity (as she calls it elsewhere), that she had good reason to worry throughout the sonnet sequence about the effect of her own sadness on Robert. Sonnet 5 is eerily prophetic. The Brownings were to have a happy marriage of fifteen years. But in the last years of her life, Elizabeth became haunted by the death of her father, who would never forgive her for marrying, and by the death of her sister Henrietta, whom the father also never forgave for later marrying. The ashes of her morbidity ignited once more, and she valiantly struggled against a lingering depression that Robert could no longer stamp out.

The lover not considering herself worthy of the beloved is not simply a poetic convention in these sonnets — the first in the tradition in which a woman poet addresses the male. Her sadness and ill health are the very facts of her existence. Does her love of Robert demand that she renounce him for his sake? In the first four sonnets she assumes it does. What has Robert to do with "a poor, tired, wandering singer" like her? The disparity between them is too great. In Sonnets 6 to 9 her ambivalence is evident: "I only love thee! let it pass."

And Love Is Fire

The unsettling image that ends Sonnet 8 gives the reader an uneasy glimpse of the lack of self-esteem that plagued her after the death of Bro:

> For frequent tears have run
> The colours from my life, and left so dead
> And pale a stuff, it were not fitly done
> To give the same as pillow to thy head.
> Go farther! let it serve to trample on.

In Sonnet 10 she realizes that "There's nothing low | In love." God loves his "meanest creatures," so therefore even her "mere love is beautiful indeed | And worthy of acceptation." There's a rather hallucinatory glow to the imagery, as there often is when the two lovers face one another:

> Fire is bright,
> Let temple burn, or flax. An equal light
> Leaps in the flame from cedar-plank or weed.
> And love is fire; and when I say at need
> I love thee .. mark! .. I love thee! .. in thy sight
> I stand transfigured, glorified aright,
> With conscience of the new rays that proceed
> Out of my face toward thine.

In Sonnet 11 she continues this theme of transfiguration, but in the end comes back to her ambivalence and again is ready to renounce her lover — although in Sonnet 12 she boasts of her love. Sonnet 13 and 15 are interesting, as they both seem to arise out of Robert's visits to her, always in the afternoon when Moulton Barrett was at work. During their time together he must have asked her to "fashion into speech | The love I bear thee." And he must have wondered out loud not only at her silence but also, during another visit, at her "Too calm and sad a face." Certainly he would have wondered less and worried more if he had been privy to Sonnets 13 and 15.

It is in Sonnet 14 that she speaks in a more assured and confident voice, reiterating a theme that runs all through the love letters. "If thou must love me, let it be for nought | Except for love's sake only." Elizabeth's letters this issue can be as witty as the sonnet is serious. Both lovers know that to an outsider it might look as if each were enamored of the other's accomplishments – or supposed virtues. But for them, true love is unconditional – one loves because one loves. What the world usually calls love is really a form of ego gratification that can as easily turn to hate (Sonnet 40) – *male* ego gratification, if one reads her outspoken letters on the subject.

There is a sense of play in Sonnets 18 and 19, which deal with exchanging locks of hair. And in Sonnet 20 the poet remembers what the world was like without Robert. From then on, cherished details from the courtship are seen in the poems, and in Sonnets 22–24 there's more of an insistence upon living in the world. As she says in Sonnet 23, "I yield the grave for thy sake." Sonnets 26 and 27 offer a haunting portrayal of her earlier life ("I lived with visions for my company"), as do Sonnets 33 and 34, where she implores Robert, "Yes, call me by my pet-name!" That name "Ba," given to her in childhood by her darling Bro, was what all of her family and friends called her throughout her life. As with lovers before and after, the memory of every phase of their love is now bringing its own pleasure. In Sonnet 28 she rereads Robert's letters, counting out each stage in their love. There is an erotic undercurrent to Sonnet 29, when her thoughts become the "wild vines" encircling him, her "palm-tree," her "strong tree," shattering her "bands of greenery" and exposing once more "thy trunk all bare." The memory of their first kiss is equally evocative in Sonnet 38.

Sonnet 41 was written close to her secret marriage. It has the tone of a valedictory address delivered to the world. Within the confines of her room and her imagination, she thanks all who have loved her, all who paused near her "prison-wall." Almost prophetically, she feels that the way to thank Robert for his love would be

to shoot

And Love Is Fire

My soul's full meaning into future years,
That they should lend it utterance, and salute
Love that endures, from Life that disappears!

This is a poem in which an allusion to her father has been edited out be-
fore publication. The published opening, "I thank all who have loved me
in their hearts, | With thanks and love from mine," was in manuscript

I thank all who have loved me in their hearts,
Or thought they did so!

Her father's opinion and feelings were probably the reason she at first ex-
cluded from the sequence the sonnet that would later follow 41. It has
been said that she believed the opening line "My future will not copy fair
my past," which is a quote from one of her earlier poems, would give away
the fact that the sonnet sequence was autobiographical. But the lines she
might have thought would add salt to her father's wounds come later in
Sonnet 42: "I seek no copy now of life's first half: | Leave here the pages
with long musing curled." Would her father, reading them, find further
insult? She was choosing to leave Moulton Barrett and Wimpole Street,
not for Heaven, but for an entirely new and different life. This was *her*
will, *her* volition.

Sonnet 43, "How do I love thee? Let me count the ways," deserves its
curtain calls. It is the triumphant aria, the positive reevaluation and sum-
mation of the entire sequence. Yet almost quietly, in its midst, she tells
her lover,

I love thee with the passion put to use
In my old griefs, and with my childhood's faith.

The past has been redeemed, grief has been transfigured through love's
fire. "How do I love thee" in effect concludes the *Sonnets from the Portuguese.*
Her inner conflict has been resolved, her choice has been made. It is fol-
lowed by one last sonnet, one that gracefully dedicates the poems to
Robert. Sonnet 44 was written two days before the couple's secret mar-

riage on September 12, 1846, and nine days before Elizabeth Barrett Browning left Wimpole Street forever.

"Nobody was ever born to be happier or unhappier than I – the 'mingled yarn' is black and white," Elizabeth Barrett Browning once wrote to a friend. This was no more poetic hyperbole than the fact that the choice the poet faced in 1845 was that between love and death.

It was a tremendous act of courage for this brilliant poet and dutiful daughter to be the first child to disobey her father's wishes and marry – particularly if she had, as well, some secret understanding of why he did not wish to have any of his children marry or to have any legitimate grandchildren to carry on the Moulton Barrett name. The Barretts were a Creole family, and most of Moulton Barrett's illegitimate first cousins had mixed blood, as did Moulton Barret's own absent father, Charles Moulton. Both Edward Barrett Moulton Barrett and his abolitionist daughter Elizabeth were quite dark-skinned. As I have shown in my biography of the Brownings' marriage, *Dared and Done* (Knopf, 1995), it is more than likely that, in his secretive and tortured way, Moulton Barrett was attempting to end his line because of his mixed blood. His unexpressed Nonconformist guilt on the issue of slavery, as well as his lot as a Creole living in a country that now despised the colonial planters, added to his peculiarities.

"Cursed we are from generation to generation," Moulton Barrett often said. Literally as well as figuratively the mingled yarn of Elizabeth Barrett Browning's life was black and white – and she was well aware of it. The sufferings she refers to time and again in the sonnets include deaths that are psychic as well as physical. There were family issues that weighed on the heart but were not brought to the lips. She would have in marriage four miscarriages and give birth to one healthy son. The delight with which she and Robert would speak of his fair skin in letter after letter was not racist but a coded way of proving that her father's fears had been unjustified.

Elizabeth Barrett Browning's struggle not to copy life's first half led her to her own life and to a new poetry that opposed slavery in all of its forms, politically, culturally, morally. The poetry of her maturity became a call to action. This late period, in which she would produce such socially committed works as *Casa Guidi Windows* and *Aurora Leigh*, began in her bedsitting room as she wrote her letters and poems to Robert Browning: "I love thee freely, as men strive for Right."

The love letters were published by the end of the nineteenth century, and the title of the sonnets becomes even more transparent and subtly ironic when the poems are now, for the first time, read in concert with the letters. *She* was the Portuguese. In love with one who had a "princely Heart," in the *Sonnets from the Portuguese* Elizabeth Barrett Browning chose life over death and found her own path to action.

A Note on Sources

BY WILLIAM S. PETERSON

SONNETS FROM THE PORTUGUESE was first published in Elizabeth Barret Browning's *Poems* (1850) and was reprinted, with revisions, in her *Poems* (1856). It exists in three surviving manuscripts: the Pierpont Morgan Library version, the earliest, is incomplete; the British Library manuscript is the intermediate draft that remained in Robert Browning's possession; and the Armstrong Browning Library (Baylor University) manuscript, formerly owned by Arthur A. Houghton, Jr., served as printer's copy in 1850.

We have examined the manuscripts and in a few instances have noted significant details in them, but for our text we have followed the published version of 1856, the last that Elizabeth (who died in 1861) was able to supervise. We have made a few minor modifications in the 1856 text. We have changed the sonnet numbers from roman to arabic numerals. In Sonnet 20, line 8, we have removed one of the periods from an ellipsis of four periods, because elsewhere, both in her poetry and letters, Elizabeth uses groups of two or three periods but never four. We have also removed the grave accent from *belovèd*, since the accent does not appear in the manuscripts of the poem, and her printers were inconsistent in applying it. The rhythm of the lines makes it self-evident that Elizabeth intended *beloved* to be pronounced as a three-syllable word.

The older standard edition of Elizabeth's poems was edited by Charlotte Porter and Helen Clarke (6 volumes, New York, 1900). There is no satisfactory modern collection, but three twentieth-century editions of the *Sonnets from the Portuguese* contain important textual information: the Centennial Vari-

A Note on Sources

orum Edition by Fannie Ratchford (New York, 1950), the variorum edition by Miroslava Wein Dow (Troy, N.Y., 1980), and the fascimile edition of the British Library manuscript by William S. Peterson (Barre, Mass., 1977).

The passages from the love letters between Robert and Elizabeth are taken from *The Letters of Robert Browning and Elizabeth Barrett Barrett 1845–1846*, edited by Elvan Kintner (2 volumes, Cambridge, Mass., 1969). The original letters are in the Margaret Clapp Library, Wellesley College. The letter on page 91 is quoted from *Robert Browning and Julia Wedgwood: A Broken Friendship as Revealed by Their Letters*, edited by Richard Curle (New York, 1937).

Because both Robert and Elizabeth frequently use ellipses in their letters, we have indicated our own omissions by three periods within brackets.

Acknowledgments

W E are indebted to the Margaret Clapp Library, Wellesley College, for permission to quote passages from the Brownings' love letters, and to the Armstrong Browning Library, Baylor University, for furnishing a photocopy of the *Sonnets from the Portuguese* as published in Elizabeth Barrett Browning's *Poems* (1856).

In addition, we wish to thank Dr. Roger Brooks and Rita Humphrey at the Armstrong Browning Library, Ruth Rodgers and Jill Triplett at the Margaret Clapp Library, and Marilyn Palmeri at the Pierpont Morgan Library for their assistance and prompt attention to questions raised and materials requested. We are grateful to Harriet Wasserman for her enthusiasm, suggestions, and support, and to Michael Montlack for his reading of the introduction and an early draft of the text. Finally, we wish to thank Captain Gordon E. Moulton-Barrett, who generously allowed us to see — and to publish for the first time in this edition — Elizabeth's sketch of the view from her window at Bagni di Lucca.

ILLUSTRATION CREDITS: frontispiece, 26, The Pierpont Morgan Library, New York (MA 933); 8, 34, 66, Special Collections, Margaret Clapp Library, Wellesley College; 70, 82 (Elizabeth Barrett), Eton College Library; 82 (Robert Browning), engraving by J. C. Armytage in Richard Hengist Horne's *A New Spirit of the Age* (London, 1844); 90, Captain Gordon E. Moulton-Barrett.

Sonnets from the Portuguese

෨ *Robert to Elizabeth (his first letter to her)*

I love your verses with all my heart, dear Miss Barrett, – and this is no off-hand complimentary letter that I shall write, – whatever else, no prompt matter-of-course recognition of your genius, and there a graceful and natural end of the thing: since the day last week when I first read your poems, I quite laugh to remember how I have been turning and turning again in my mind what I should be able to tell you of their effect upon me. [. . .] Into me has it gone, and part of me has it become, this great living poetry of yours. [. . .] I can give a reason for my faith in one and another excellence, the fresh strange music, the affluent language, the exquisite pathos and true new brave thought – but in this addressing myself to you – your own true self, and for the first time, my feeling rises altogether. I do, as I say, love these books with all my heart – and I love you too: do you know I was once not very far from seeing – really seeing you? [. . .] You were too unwell – and now it is years ago – and I feel as at some untoward passage in my travels – as if I had been close, so close, to some world's-wonder in chapel or crypt, only a screen to push and I might have entered, but there was some slight . . so it now seems . . slight and just-sufficient bar to admission; and the half-opened door shut, and I went home my thousands of miles, and the sight was never to be!

Well, these Poems were to be – and this true thankful joy and pride with which I feel myself

Yours ever faithfully,

Robert Browning

෨ *Elizabeth to Robert (her first letter to him)*

I thank you, dear Mr. Browning, from the bottom of my heart. [...] Sympathy is dear – very dear to me: but the sympathy of a poet, & of such a poet, is the quintessence of sympathy to me!

[...] BUT . . . you know . . if you had entered the 'crypt,' you might have caught cold, or been tired to death, & *wished* yourself 'a thousand miles off' – which would have been worse than travelling them. It is not my interest however to put such thoughts in your head about its' being "all for the best" – and I would rather hope (as I do) that what I lost by one chance I may recover by some future one. Winters shut me up as they do dormouse's eyes: in the spring, *we shall see.*

January 13, 1845

෨ *Robert to Elizabeth*

See how I go on and on to you, – I who, whenever now and then pulled, by the head and hair, into letter-writing, get sorrowfully on for a line or two. [. . .] I will joyfully wait for the delight of your friendship, and the spring, and my Chapel-sight after all!

I

I thought once how Theocritus had sung
Of the sweet years, the dear and wished for years,
Who each one in a gracious hand appears
To bear a gift for mortals, old or young:
And, as I mused it in his antique tongue,
I saw, in gradual vision through my tears,
The sweet, sad years, the melancholy years,
Those of my own life, who by turns had flung
A shadow across me. Straightway I was 'ware,
So weeping, how a mystic Shape did move
Behind me, and drew me backward by the hair;
And a voice said in mastery while I strove, . .
'Guess now who holds thee?'—'Death!' I said. But there,
The silver answer rang . . 'Not Death, but Love.'

Sonnet 2 was originally entitled "Love's Obstacles."

❧ *Elizabeth to Robert*

If I were different in some respects [*her health*] and free in others [*her father*], [. . .] I would accept. [. . .] I *would* do it . . *not, I do* . . observe!

❧ *Robert to Elizabeth*

I understand you to signify to me that you see, at this present, insurmountable obstacles. [. . .] I thank God – I *do* thank him, that in this whole matter I have been, to the utmost of my power, not unworthy of his introducing you to me, [. . .] having for many years now made up my mind to the impossibility of loving any woman . . having wondered at this in the beginning, and fought not a little against in, having acquiesced in it at last, and accounted for it all to myself, and become, if anything, rather proud of it than sorry . . I say, when real love, making itself at once recognized as such, *did* reveal itself to me at last, I *did* open my heart to it with a cry.

❧ 2 ❧

But only three in all God's universe
Have heard this word thou hast said, — Himself, beside
Thee speaking, and me listening! and replied
One of us .. that was God, .. and laid the curse
So darkly on my eyelids, as to amerce
My sight from seeing thee, — that if I had died,
The deathweights, placed there, would have signified
Less absolute exclusion. 'Nay' is worse
From God than from all others, O my friend!
Men could not part us with their worldly jars,
Nor the seas change us, nor the tempests bend;
Our hands would touch for all the mountain-bars, —
And, heaven being rolled between us at the end,
We should but vow the faster for the stars.

ॐ *Robert to Elizabeth*

   I heard of you, dear Miss Barrett, between a Polka and a Cellarius the other evening, of Mr. Kenyon.

ॐ *Elizabeth to Robert*

   As to the Polkas and Cellariuses, . . I do not covet them of course . . but what a strange world you seem to have, to me at a distance — what a strange husk of a world! How it looks to me like mandarin-life or something as remote.

ॐ *Elizabeth to Robert*

   Do you remember when you wrote first to me *"May God bless you & me in that!"* It was before we met. Can you guess what I thought? — I have the whole effect in my memory distinctly. I felt with a bitter feeling, that it was quite a pity to throw away such beautiful words out of the window into the dark.

Unlike are we, unlike, O princely Heart!
Unlike our uses and our destinies.
Our ministering two angels look surprise
On one another, as they strike athwart
Their wings in passing. Thou, bethink thee, art
A guest for queens to social pageantries,
With gages from a hundred brighter eyes
Than tears even can make mine, to ply thy part
Of chief musician. What hast thou to do
With looking from the lattice-lights at me,
A poor, tired, wandering singer, . . . singing through
The dark, and leaning up a cypress tree?
The chrism is on thine head, — on mine, the dew, —
And Death must dig the level where these agree.

The door of 50 Wimpole Street, London, through which Robert's letters to Elizabeth passed. After this photograph was taken, the door was restored and installed in the Margaret Clapp Library, Wellesley College.

4

Thou has thy calling to some palace-floor,
Most gracious singer of high poems! where
The dancers will break footing, from the care
Of watching up thy pregnant lips for more.
And dost thou lift this house's latch too poor
For hand of thine? and canst thou think and bear
To let thy music drop here unaware
In folds of golden fulness at my door?
Look up and see the casement broken in,
The bats and owlets builders in the roof!
My cricket chirps against thy mandolin.
Hush, call no echo up in further proof
Of desolation! there's a voice within
That weeps . . as thou must sing . . alone, aloof.

Electra attempted to bury her brother. The ashes Elizabeth overturned at Robert's feet were her grief and guilt about the death of her beloved brother Edward (Bro) in 1840. This was the first time, after five years, that she had been able to speak of it.

August 20, 1845

❧ *Elizabeth to Robert*

They sent me down you know to Torquay [*for her health*] – Dr. Chambers saying that I could not live a winter in London – The worst . . – what people call the worst – was apprehended for me at that time. So I was sent down with my sister to my aunt there – and he, my brother whom I loved so, was sent too, to take us there & return. And when the time came for him to leave me, [. . .] *I*, weakened by illness, could not master my spirits or drive back my tears – & my aunt kissed them away instead of reproving me as she should have done; & said that *she* would take care that I should not be grieved . . *she!* . . and so she sate down & wrote a letter to Papa to tell him that he would "break my heart" if he persisted in calling away my brother – As if hearts were broken *so!* [. . .] And Papa's answer was – burnt into me, as with fire, it is – that "under such circumstances he did not refuse to suspend his purpose, but that he considered it to be *very wrong in me to exact such a thing.*" So there was no separation *then:* & month after month passed – & sometimes I was better & sometimes worse – & the medical men continued to say that they would not answer for my life . . they! if I were agitated – & so there was no more talk of a separation. And once *he* held my hand, . . how I remember! & said that he "loved me better than them all & that he *would not* leave me . . till I was well." [. . .] And ten days from that day the boat had left the shore which never returned; never – & he *had* left me! gone! For three days we waited – & I hoped while I could – oh – that awful agony of three days! And the sun shone as it shines to-day, & there was no more wind than now; and the sea under the windows was like this paper for smoothness – & my sisters drew the curtains back that I might see for myself how smooth the sea was, & how it could hurt nobody – & other boats came back one by one.

❧ 5 ❧

I lift my heavy heart up solemnly,
As once Electra her sepulchral urn,
And, looking in thine eyes, I overturn
The ashes at thy feet. Behold and see
What a great heap of grief lay hid in me,
And how the red wild sparkles dimly burn
Through the ashen greyness. If thy foot in scorn
Could tread them out to darkness utterly,
It might be well perhaps. But if instead
Thou wait beside me for the wind to blow
The grey dust up, . . . those laurels on thine head,
O my beloved, will not shield thee so,
That none of all the fires shall scorch and shred
The hair beneath. Stand further off then! go.

ॐ *Robert to Elizabeth*

I believe in you absolutely, utterly – I believe that when you bade me, that time, be silent [*about his love*], – that such was your bidding, and I was silent. [. . .] Let me say now – *this only once* – that I loved you from my soul, and gave you my life, so much of it as you would take, – and all that is *done*, not to be altered now.

ॐ *Elizabeth to Robert*

Your life! . . if you gave it to me & I put my whole heart into it; what should I put but anxiety, & more sadness than you were born to? What could I give you, which it would not be ungenerous to give? Therefore we must leave this subject – & I must trust you to leave it without one word more; too many have been said already.

ॐ *Elizabeth to Robert*

Think of your very own, who bids God bless you when she prays for herself! –

6

Go from me. Yet I feel that I shall stand
Henceforward in thy shadow. Nevermore
Alone upon the threshold of my door
Of individual life, I shall command
The uses of my soul, nor lift my hand
Serenely in the sunshine as before,
Without the sense of that which I forbore, . .
Thy touch upon the palm. The widest land
Doom takes to part us, leaves thy heart in mine
With pulses that beat double. What I do
And what I dream include thee, as the wine
Must taste of its own grapes. And when I sue
God for myself, He hears that name of thine,
And sees within my eyes, the tears of two.

September 17, 1845

૨➤ *Elizabeth to Robert*

I had done *living,* I thought, when you came & sought me out!

April 15, 1845

૨➤ *Robert to Elizabeth*

One of these days I shall describe a country I have seen in my soul only, fruits, flowers, birds and all.

Ever yours, dear Miss Barrett,

R. Browning

June 3, 1846

૨➤ *Elizabeth to Robert*

I shudder to look back to the days when you were not for me. Was ever life so like death before? My face was so close against the tombstones, that there seemed no room even for the tears.

7

The face of all the world is changed, I think,
  Since first I heard the footsteps of thy soul
  Move still, oh, still, beside me, as they stole
  Betwixt me and the dreadful outer brink
Of obvious death, where I, who thought to sink,
  Was caught up into love, and taught the whole
  Of life in a new rhythm. The cup of dole
  God gave for baptism, I am fain to drink,
And praise its sweetness, Sweet, with thee anear.
  The names of country, heaven, are changed away
  For where thou art or shalt be, there or here;
And this . . this lute and song . . loved yesterday,
  (The singing angels know) are only dear,
Because thy name moves right in what they say.

ᘓ *Robert to Elizabeth*

If turned to gold, I WOULD not even then desire to become more
than the mere setting to *that* diamond you must always wear: the re-
gard and esteem you now give me, in this letter, and which I press to
my heart & bow my head upon, is all I can take & all too embarrass-
ing.

ᘓ *Robert to Elizabeth*

Let me count my gold now – and rub off any speck that stays the
full shining. [. . .] Oh, *how* I love you when I think of the entire
truthfulness of your generosity to me – how, meaning, and willing
to *give*, you gave *nobly!* Do you think I have not seen in this world
how women who *do* love will manage to confer that gift on occa-
sion? And shall I allow myself to fancy how much alloy such pure
gold as *your* love would have rendered endurable? – Yet it came, vir-
gin ore, to complete my fortune!

8

What can I give thee back, O liberal
And princely giver, who has brought the gold
And purple of thine heart, unstained, untold,
And laid them on the outside of the wall
For such as I to take or leave withal,
In unexpected largesse? am I cold,
Ungrateful, that for these most manifold
High gifts, I render nothing back at all?
Not so; not cold, — but very poor instead.
Ask God who knows. For frequent tears have run
The colours from my life, and left so dead
And pale a stuff, it were not fitly done
To give the same as pillow to thy head.
Go farther! let it serve to trample on.

෫෯ *Elizabeth to Robert*

I write one word just to say that it is all over with Pisa [*where she was to have gone for her health*]: which was a probable evil when I wrote last, & which I foresaw from the beginning – being a prophetess, you know. I cannot tell you now how it has all happened – *only do not blame me,* for I have kept my ground to the last, & only yield when Mr. Kenyon & all the world see that there is no standing. I am ashamed almost of having put so much earnestness into a personal matter – & I spoke face to face [*to her father, urging him to let her go*] & quite firmly – so as to pass with my sisters for the "bravest person in the house" without contestation.

෫෯ *Elizabeth to Robert*

But one word before we leave the subject, and then to leave it finally. [. . .] The "insurmountable" difficulty is for you & everybody to see, – – & for me to feel, who have been a very byword among the talkers, for a confirmed invalid through months & years, & who, even if I were going to Pisa & had the best prospects possible to me, should yet remain liable to relapses & stand on precarious ground to the end of my life. Now that is no mystery for the trying of "faith"; but a plain fact, which neither thinking nor speaking can make less a fact. But DON'T let us speak of it.

9

Can it be right to give what I can give?
To let thee sit beneath the fall of tears
As salt as mine, and hear the sighing years
Re-sighing on my lips renunciative
Through those infrequent smiles which fail to live
For all thy adjurations? O my fears,
That this can scarce be right! We are not peers,
So to be lovers; and I own, and grieve,
That givers of such gifts as mine are, must
Be counted with the ungenerous. Out, alas!
I will not soil thy purple with my dust,
Nor breathe my poison on thy Venice-glass,
Nor give thee any love . . . which were unjust.
Beloved, I only love thee! let it pass.

& *I Timothy 4:9*

This is a faithful saying and worthy of all acceptation.

September 18, 1845

& *Robert to Elizabeth*

I desire in this life [. . .] to live and just write out certain things which are in me, and so save my soul. I would endeavour to do this if I were forced to "live among lions" as you once said – but I should best do this if I lived quietly with myself and with you. That you cannot dance like Cerito does not materially disarrange this plan – nor that I might (beside the perpetual incentive and sustainment and consolation) get, over and above the main reward, the incidental, particular and unexpected happiness of being allowed when not working to rather occupy myself with watching you, that with certain other pursuits I might be otherwise addicted to – *this*, also, does not constitute an obstacle, as I see obstacles – [. . .]

God bless you, dearest friend.

R. B.

❦ IO ❧

Yet, love, mere love, is beautiful indeed
And worthy of acceptation. Fire is bright,
Let temple burn, or flax. An equal light
Leaps in the flame from cedar-plank or weed.
And love is fire; and when I say at need
I love thee .. mark! .. I love thee! .. in thy sight
I stand transfigured, glorified aright,
With conscience of the new rays that proceed
Out of my face toward thine. There's nothing low
In love, when love the lowest: meanest creatures
Who love God, God accepts while loving so.
And what I feel, across the inferior features
Of what I am, doth flash itself, and show
How that great work of Love enhances Nature's.

ॐ *Robert to Elizabeth*

I should have been proud beyond measure & happy past all desert, to call and be allowed to see you simply, speak with you and be spoken to – what am I more than others? Don't think this mock humility – *it is not* – you take me in your mantle, and we shine together, but I know my part in it! All this is written breathlessly on a sudden fancy that you *might* . . if not now, at some future time – , give other than this, the true reason, for that discrepancy you see, that nearness in the letters, that early farness in the visits! And, love, all love is but a passionate *drawing closer* – I would be one with you, dearest, – let my soul press close to you, as my lips, dear life of my life –

►§ II ◄

And therefore if to love can be desert,
I am not all unworthy. Cheeks as pale
As those you see, and trembling knees that fail
To bear the burden of a heavy heart, —
This weary minstrel-life that once was girt
To climb Aornus, and can scarce avail
To pipe now 'gainst the valley nightingale
A melancholy music, — why advert
To these things? O Beloved, it is plain
I am not of thy worth nor for thy place!
And yet, because I love thee, I obtain
From that same love this vindicating grace,
To live on still in love, and yet in vain, . .
To bless thee, yet renounce thee to thy face.

ঌ *Robert to Elizabeth*

I think I ought to understand what a father may exact, and a child should comply with – and I respect the most ambiguous of love's caprices. [. . .] Did I, when you signified to me the probable objections [. . .] to myself, my own happiness, – did I once allude to . . much less argue against, or refuse to acknowledge those objections? For I wholly sympathize, however it go against me, with the highest, wariest, pride & love for you, and the proper jealousy and vigilance they entail – but now, and here, the jewel is not being over guarded, but ruined, cast away [*by her father's refusal to allow her to go to Pisa for her health*]. And whoever is privileged to interfere should do so in the possessor's own interest – all common sense interferes – all rationality against absolute no-reason at all.

12

Indeed this very love which is my boast,
And which, when rising up from breast to brow,
Doth crown me with a ruby large enow
To draw men's eyes and prove the inner cost, . .
This love even, all my worth, to the uttermost,
I should not love withal, unless that thou
Hadst set me an example, shown me how,
When first thine earnest eyes with mine were crossed,
And love called love. And thus, I cannot speak
Of love even, as a good thing of my own.
Thy soul hath snatched up mine all faint and weak,
And placed it by thee on a golden throne, —
And that I love (O soul, we must be meek!)
Is by thee only, whom I love alone.

Sonnet 13, from the earliest surviving manuscript of the *Sonnets from the Portuguese*, now in the Pierpont Morgan Library, New York.

❦ 13 ❧

And wilt thou have me fashion into speech
The love I bear thee, finding words enough,
And hold the torch out, while the winds are rough,
Between our faces, to cast light on each? —
I drop it at thy feet. I cannot teach
My hand to hold my spirit so far off
From myself .. me .. that I should bring thee proof
In words, of love hid in me out of reach.
Nay, let the silence of my womanhood
Commend my woman-love to thy belief, —
Seeing that I stand unwon, however wooed,
And rend the garment of my life, in brief,
By a most dauntless, voiceless fortitude,
Lest one touch of this heart convey its grief.

October 23, 1845

❧ *Robert to Elizabeth*

I love you because I *love* you; I see you "once a week" because I cannot see you all day long; I think of you all day long, because I most certainly could not think of you once an hour less, if I tried, or went to Pisa, or "abroad" (in every sense) in order to 'be happy'.

October 24, 1845

❧ *Elizabeth to Robert*

I have sometimes felt jealous of myself . . of my own infirmities, . . and thought that you cared for me only because your chivalry touched them with a silver sound – & that, without them, you would pass by on the other side: – why twenty times I have thought *that* & been vexed – ungrateful vexation!

November 12, 1845

❧ *Elizabeth to Robert*

The first moment in which I seemed to admit to myself in a flash of lightning the *possibility* of your affection for me being more than dream-work . . the first moment was *that* when you intimated (as you have done since repeatedly) that you cared for me not for a reason, but because you cared for me.

May 11, 1846

❧ *Elizabeth to Robert*

So you think that I meant to complain when we first met, of your *"loving me only for my poetry"!* [. . .] I am not over-particular, I fancy, about what I may be loved for. There is no good reason for loving me, certainly, & my earnest desire (as I have said again & again) is, that there should be by profession no reason at all. But if there is to be any sort of reason, why one is as welcome as another . . you may love me for my shoes, if you like it . . except that they wear out.

14

If thou must love me, let it be for nought
Except for love's sake only. Do not say
'I love her for her smile . . her look . . her way
Of speaking gently, . . for a trick of thought
That falls in well with mine, and certes brought
A sense of pleasant ease on such a day'—
For these things in themselves, Beloved, may
Be changed, or change for thee, — and love, so wrought,
May be unwrought so. Neither love me for
Thine own dear pity's wiping my cheeks dry, —
A creature might forget to weep, who bore
Thy comfort long, and lose thy love thereby!
But love me for love's sake, that evermore
Thou may'st love on, through love's eternity.

࿊ *Elizabeth to Robert*

It is not 'misunderstanding' you to know you to be the most gen-
erous & loyal of all in the world – you overwhelm me with your
generosity – only while you see from above & I from below, we can-
not see the same thing in the same light. Moreover, if we DID, I
should be more beneath you in one sense, than I am. Do me the jus-
tice of remembering this whenever you recur in thought to the sub-
ject which ends here in the words of it. [. . .]

I am yours, E. B. B.

࿊ *Elizabeth to Robert*

I am frightened . . I tremble! When you come to know me as well
as I know myself, what can save me, do you think, from disappoint-
ing & displeasing you? I ask the question, & find no answer –

❧15❧

Accuse me not, beseech thee, that I wear
Too calm and sad a face in front of thine;
For we two look two ways, and cannot shine
With the same sunlight on our brow and hair.
On me thou lookest, with no doubting care,
As on a bee shut in a crystalline, —
Since sorrow hath shut me safe in love's divine,
And to spread wing and fly in the outer air
Were most impossible failure, if I strove
To fail so. But I look on thee .. on thee ..
Beholding, besides love, the end of love,
Hearing oblivion beyond memory!
As one who sits and gazes from above,
Over the rivers to the bitter sea.

꙳ *Robert to Elizabeth*

All our life is some form of religion, and all our action some be-lief. [. . .] In your case I do think you are called upon to do your duty to yourself; that is, to God in the end. [. . .] Will it not be infinitely harder to act so than to blindly adopt his [*her father's*] pleasure, and die under it? Who can not do that?

[. . .] I would marry you now and thus – I would come when you let me, and go when you bade me – I would be no more than one of your brothers – *"no more"* – that is, instead of getting to-morrow for Saturday, I should get Saturday as well – two hours for one – when your head ached I should be *here*.

September 26, 1845

꙳ *Elizabeth to Robert*

Henceforward I am yours for everything but to do you harm – and I am yours too much, in my heart, ever to consent to do you harm in that way. [. . .] However this may be, a promise goes to you in it that none, except God & your will, shall interpose between you & me, . . I mean, that if He should free me within a moderate time from the trailing chain of this weakness, I will then be to you what-ever at that hour you shall choose . . whether friend or more than friend . . a friend to the last in any case. So it rests with God & with you.

16

And yet, because thou overcomest so,
Because thou art more noble and like a king,
Thou canst prevail against my fears and fling
Thy purple round me, till my heart shall grow
Too close against thine heart, henceforth to know
How it shook when alone. Why, conquering
May prove as lordly and complete a thing
In lifting upward, as in crushing low!
And as a vanquished soldier yields his sword
To one who lifts him from the bloody earth, —
Even so, Beloved, I at last record,
Here ends my strife. If thou invite me forth,
I rise above abasement at the word.
Make thy love larger to enlarge my worth.

ॐ *Robert to Elizabeth*

I do solemnly, unaffectedly wonder how you can put so much
pure felicity into an envelope so as that I shall get it as from the
fount head. This to-day, those yesterday – there is, I see, and know,
thus much goodness in line after line, goodness to be scientifically
appreciated, *proved there* – but over and above, is it in the writing,
the dots and traces, the seal, the paper, – here does the subtle charm
lie beyond all rational accounting for? The other day I stumbled on
a quotation from J. Baptista Porta – wherein he avers that any musi-
cal instrument made out of wood possessed of medicinal properties
retains, being put to use, such virtues undiminished, – and that, for
instance, a sick man to whom you should pipe on a pipe of elder-
tree would so receive all the advantage derivable from a decoction
of its berries. From whence, by a parity of reasoning, I may discover,
I think, that the very ink and paper were . . ah, what were they?

March 7, 1846

ॐ *Robert to Elizabeth*

For music, I made myself melancholy just now with some "Con-
certos for the Harpsichord by Mr. Handel."

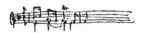

❦17❦

My poet, thou canst touch on all the notes
God set between His After and Before,
And strike up and strike off the general roar
Of the rushing worlds, a melody that floats
In a serene air purely. Antidotes
Of medicated music, answering for
Mankind's forlornest uses, thou canst pour
From thence into their ears. God's will devotes
Thine to such ends, and mine to wait on thine.
How, Dearest, wilt thou have me for most use?
A hope, to sing by gladly? . . or a fine
Sad memory, with thy songs to interfuse?
A shade, in which to sing . . . of palm or pine?
A grave, on which to rest from singing? . . Choose.

᛭ *Robert to Elizabeth*

Give me, dearest beyond expression, what I have always dared to think I would ask you for . . one day! Give me [. . .] so much of you – all precious that you are – as may be given in a lock of your hair.

᛭ *Elizabeth to Robert*

I never gave away what you ask me to give *you*, to a human being, except my nearest relatives & once or twice or thrice to female friends, . . never, though reproached for it, – and it is just three weeks since I said last to an asker that I was "too great a prude for such a thing"! it was best to anticipate the accusation! – And, prude or not, I could not – I never could – *something* would not let me.

᛭ *Robert to Elizabeth*

Take it, dearest, – what I am forced to think you mean – and take *no more* with it – for I gave all to give long ago – I am all yours – and now, *mine*, – give me *mine* to be happy with!

✤18✤

I never gave a lock of hair away
To a man, Dearest, except this to thee,
Which now upon my fingers thoughtfully
I ring out to the full brown length and say
'Take it.' My day of youth went yesterday;
My hair no longer bounds to my foot's glee,
Nor plant I it from rose or myrtle-tree,
As girls do, any more. It only may
Now shade on two pale cheeks, the mark of tears,
Taught drooping from the head that hangs aside
Through sorrow's trick. I thought the funeral-shears
Would take this first, but Love is justified, —
Take it thou, . . finding pure, from all those years,
The kiss my mother left here when she died.

November 24, 1845

🕊 *Elizabeth to Robert*

Now you must not blame me – you must not. To make a promise is one thing, & to keep it, quite another. [. . .] I am not to blame for saying now . . (listen!) that I *never can* nor *will give you this thing;* – only that I will, if you please, exchange it for another thing – you understand. I too will avoid being 'assuming'; I will not pretend to be generous, no, nor "kind." It shall be pure merchandise or nothing at all.

November 28, 1845

🕊 *Elizabeth to Robert*

It comes at eight oclock – the post says eight . . *I* say near half past eight . . : it *comes* and I thank you, thank you, as I can. Do you remember the purple lock of a king on which hung the fate of a city? *I* do! And I need not in conscience – because this one here did not come to me by treason – [I and my king] on the contrary, do fairly give & take.

❧19❧

The soul's Rialto hath its merchandise;
  I barter curl for curl upon that mart,
 And from my poet's forehead to my heart,
Receive this lock which outweighs argosies, —
   As purply black, as erst, to Pindar's eyes,
  The dim purpureal tresses gloomed athwart
The nine white Muse-brows. For this counterpart, . .
   Thy bay-crown's shade, Beloved, I surmise,
    Still lingers on thy curl, it is so black!
 Thus, with a fillet of smooth-kissing breath,
   I tie the shadow safe from gliding back,
 And lay the gift where nothing hindereth,
Here on my heart, as on thy brow, to lack
No natural heat till mine grows cold in death.

❧ *Elizabeth to Robert (written on the anniversary of his first letter to her)*

Shall I tell you? – it seems to me, to myself, that no man was ever before to any woman what you are to me – the fulness must be in proportion, you know, to the vacancy . . & only I know what was behind . . the long wilderness *without* the footstep . . without the blossoming rose . . and the capacity for happiness, like a black gaping hole, before this silver flooding.

May 19, 1846

❧ *Robert to Elizabeth (written on the anniversary of his first visit to her)*

With this day expires the first year since you have been yourself to me. [. . .] How can I thank you? [. . .] I began by loving you in comparison with all the world, – now, I love you, my Ba, in the face of your past self, as I remember it.

May 19, 1846

❧ *Elizabeth to Robert*

As to your thanking me, *that* is monstrous. [. . .] Think what I was when you saw me first . . laid there on the sofa as an object of the merest compassion! & of a sadder spirit than even the face showed! . . & then think of all your generosity & persistence in goodness. Think of it! – shall I ever cease? Not while the heart beats, which beats for you.

And now as the year has rounded itself to "the perfect round," I will speak. [. . .] I am glad now, yes, glad, . . as we were to have a miracle, . . to have it *so*, a born-miracle from the beginning.

❧ 20 ❧

Beloved, my Beloved, when I think
That thou wast in the world a year ago,
What time I sate alone here in the snow
And saw no footprint, heard the silence sink
No moment at thy voice, . . but, link by link,
Went counting all my chains, as if that so
They never could fall off at any blow
Struck by thy possible hand . . . why, thus I drink
Of life's great cup of wonder! Wonderful,
Never to feel thee thrill the day or night
With personal act or speech, — nor ever cull
Some prescience of thee with the blossoms white
Thou sawest growing! Atheists are as dull,
Who cannot guess God's presence out of sight.

෫ᴗ *Robert to Elizabeth*

And speaking of verse – somebody gave me a few days ago that Mr. Lowell's book you once mentioned to me. [. . .]

No, I will say the true thing against myself – and it is, that – when I turn from what is in my mind, and determine to write about any-body's book to avoid writing that I love & love & love again my own, dearest love – because of the cuckoo-song of it, – *then*, I shall be in no better humour with that book than with Mr. Lowell's.

May 20, 1846

෫ᴗ *Robert to Elizabeth*

My Ba, I can just kneel down to you and be kissed, – I cannot do more, nor speak, nor thank you – and I seem to have no more chance of getting new love to give you – , all is given, – so I have said before, and must keep saying now – all of me is your very own.

———————————

[. . .] Always with you in the spirit, always yearning to be with you in the body, – always, when with you, praying, as for the happi-est of fortunes, that I may remain with you for ever. So may it be, prays your

own, own R.

⛤21⛥

Say over again, and yet once over again,
That thou dost love me. Though the word repeated
Should seem 'a cuckoo-song,' as thou dost treat it,
Remember never to the hill or plain,
Valley and wood, without her cuckoo-strain,
Comes the fresh Spring in all her green completed.
Beloved, I, amid the darkness greeted
By a doubtful spirit-voice, in that doubt's pain
Cry .. 'Speak once more .. thou lovest!' Who can fear
Too many stars, though each in heaven shall roll —
Too many flowers, though each shall crown the year?
Say thou dost love me, love me, love me — toll
The silver iterance! — only minding, Dear,
To love me also in silence, with thy soul.

Exodus 25:1–2, 17–20

And the Lord spake unto Moses, saying, Speak unto the children of Israel. [. . .] And thou shalt make a mercy seat of pure gold: two cubits and a half shall be the length thereof, and a cubit and a half the breadth thereof. And thou shalt make two cherubims of gold, of beaten work shalt thou make them, in the two ends of the mercy seat. And make one cherub on the one end, and the other cherub on the other end: even of the mercy seat shall ye make the cherubims on the two ends thereof. And the cherubims shall stretch forth their wings on high, covering the mercy seat with their wings, and their faces shall look one to another; toward the mercy seat shall the faces of the cherubims be.

❧22❧

When our two souls stand up erect and strong,
Face to face, silent, drawing nigh and nigher,
Until the lengthening wings break into fire
At either curvéd point, — what bitter wrong
Can the earth do to us, that we should not long
Be here contented? Think. In mounting higher,
The angels would press on us, and aspire
To drop some golden orb of perfect song
Into our deep, dear silence. Let us stay
Rather on earth, Beloved, — where the unfit
Contrarious moods of men recoil away
And isolate pure spirits, and permit
A place to stand and love in for a day,
With darkness and the death-hour rounding it.

ॐ *Robert to Elizabeth*

I woke – late, or early – and, in one of those lucid moments when all things are thoroughly *perceived*, – whether suggested by some forgotten passage in the past sleep itself, I don't know – but I seem to *apprehend*, comprehend entirely, for the first time, what would happen if I lost you – the whole sense of that *closed door* of Catarina's came on me at once, and it was I who said – not as quoting or adapting another's words, but spontaneously, unavoidably, *'In that door, you will not enter, I have.'* And, dearest, the

Unwritten it must remain.

ॐ *From Elizabeth's "Catarina to Camoens" (1844):*

On the door you will not enter
I have gazed too long – adieu!
Hope withdraws her peradventure –
Death is near me, – and not you.

ॐ *Elizabeth to Robert*

You stand in between me & not merely the living who stood closest, but between me & the closer graves.

❧23❧

Is it indeed so? If I lay here dead,
Would'st thou miss any life in losing mine?
And would the sun for thee more coldly shine,
Because of grave-damps falling round my head?
I marvelled, my Beloved, when I read
Thy thought so in the letter. I am thine —
But . . so much to thee? Can I pour thy wine
While my hands tremble? Then my soul, instead
Of dreams of death, resumes life's lower range.
Then, love me, Love! look on me . . breathe on me!
As brighter ladies do not count it strange,
For love, to give up acres and degree,
I yield the grave for thy sake, and exchange
My near sweet view of Heaven, for earth with thee!

❧ *Elizabeth to Robert*

The peculiarity of our circumstances [*Elizabeth was wealthier than Robert*] will enable us to be free of the world . . of our friends even . . of all observation & examination, in certain respects: now let us use the advantage which falls to us from our misfortune, – &, since we must act for ourselves at last, let us resist the curiosity of the whole race of third persons . . even the affectionate interest of such friends as dear Mr. Kenyon, . . & put it into the power of nobody to say to himself or to another, . . "She had so much, & he, so much, in worldly possessions – or she had not so much & he had not so much." Try to understand what I mean. As it is not the least importance to either of us, as long as we can live, whether the sixpence, we live by, came most from you or from me . . & as it will be as much mine as your, & yours as mine, when we are together . . why let us join in throwing a little dust in all the winking eyes round – oh, it is nonsense & weakness, I know – but I would rather, rather, see winking eyes than staring eyes. What has anybody to do with us? Even my own family . . why should they *ever* see the farthest figure of *our* affairs, as to mere money?

24

Let the world's sharpness like a clasping knife
Shut in upon itself and do no harm
In this close hand of Love, now soft and warm,
And let us hear no sound of human strife
After the click of the shutting. Life to life —
I lean upon thee, Dear, without alarm,
And feel as safe as guarded by a charm
Against the stab of worldlings, who if rife
Are weak to injure. Very whitely still
The lilies of our lives may reassure
Their blossoms from their roots, accessible
Alone to heavenly dews that drop not fewer;
Growing straight, out of man's reach, on the hill.
God only, who made us rich, can make us poor.

ɞ *Elizabeth to Robert*

You seem to have drunken of the cup of life full, with the sun shining on it. I have lived only inwardly, – or with *sorrow*, for a strong emotion. Before this seclusion of my illness, I was secluded still – & there are few of the youngest women in the world who have not seen more, heard more, known more, of society, than I, who am scarcely to be called young now. I grew up in the country . . had no social opportunities, . . had my heart in books & poetry, . . & my experience, in reveries. My sympathies drooped towards the ground like an untrained honeysuckle – & but for *one* [*Bro*] . . in my own house . . but of this I cannot speak.

❧25❧

A heavy heart, Beloved, have I borne
From year to year until I saw thy face,
And sorrow after sorrow took the place
Of all those natural joys as lightly worn
As the stringed pearls . . each lifted in its turn
By a beating heart at dance-time. Hopes apace
Were changed to long despairs, till God's own grace
Could scarcely lift above the world forlorn
My heavy heart. Then thou didst bid me bring
And let it drop adown thy calmly great
Deep being! Fast it sinketh, as a thing
Which its own nature doth precipitate,
While thine doth close above it, mediating
Betwixt the stars and the unaccomplished fate.

&~ *Elizabeth to Robert*

It was a lonely life – growing green like the grass around it. Books and dreams were what I lived in – & domestic life only seemed to buzz gently around, like the bees around the grass. And so time passed, and passed – and afterwards, when my illness came & I seemed to stand at the edge of the world with all done, & no prospect (as appeared at one time) of ever passing the threshold of one room again, – why then, I turned to thinking with some bitterness (after the greatest sorrow of my life had given me room & time to breathe) that I had stood blind in this temple I was about to leave . . that I had seen no Human nature, that my brothers & sisters of the earth were *names* to me, . . that I had beheld no great mountain or river – nothing in fact. I was as a man dying who had not read Shakespeare . . & it was too late! – do you understand? And do you also know what a disadvantage this ignorance is to my art – Why, if I live on & yet do not escape from this seclusion, do you not perceive that I labour under signal disadvantages . . that I am, in a manner, as a *blind poet*?

26

I lived with visions for my company,
*I*nstead of men and women, years ago,
*A*nd found them gentle mates, nor thought to know
A sweeter music than they played to me.
*B*ut soon their trailing purple was not free
*O*f this world's dust, — their lutes did silent grow,
*A*nd I myself grew faint and blind below
*T*heir vanishing eyes. Then THOU didst come .. to be,
*B*eloved, what they seemed. Their shining fronts,
*T*heir songs, their splendours, (better, yet the same,
*A*s river-water hallowed into fonts)
*M*et in thee, and from out thee overcame
*M*y soul with satisfaction of all wants —
*B*ecause God's gifts put man's best dreams to shame.

From Robert's *From Robert's* The Ring and the Book (1868–69), *written after Elizabeth's death:*

O lyric Love, half-angel and half-bird
And all a wonder and a wild desire, –
Boldest of hearts that ever braved the sun,
Took sanctuary within the holier blue,
And sang a kindred soul out to his face, –
Yet human at the red-ripe of the heart.

27

My own beloved, who hast lifted me
From this drear flat of earth where I was thrown,
And, in betwixt the languid ringlets, blown
A life-breath, till the forehead hopefully
Shines out again, as all the angels see,
Before thy saving kiss! My own, my own,
Who camest to me when the world was gone,
And I who looked for only God, found thee!
I find thee; I am safe, and strong, and glad.
As one who stands in dewless asphodel,
Looks backward on the tedious time he had
In the upper life, — so I, with bosom-swell,
Make witness, here, between the good and bad,
That Love, as strong as Death, retrieves as well.

February 19, 1846

ॐ *Elizabeth to Robert*

I felt your letter to be you from the very first, & I began, from the beginning, to read every one several times over.

May 16, 1845

ॐ *Robert to Elizabeth*

Dear Miss Barrett, I thank you for the leave you give me, and for the infinite kindness of the way of giving it. I will call at 2 on Tuesday – not sooner, that you may have time to write should any adverse circumstances happen [. . .] – should you be unwell, for instance, – just send or leave word, and I will come again, and again, and again.

September 13, 1845

ॐ *Robert to Elizabeth*

I love you as you now are.

[. . .] My whole scheme of life [. . .] was long ago calculated – and it supposed *you*, the finding such an one as you, utterly impossible – because in calculating one goes upon *chances*, not on providence – how could I expect you?

September 25, 1845

ॐ *Robert to Elizabeth*

I would marry you now.

September 27, 1845

ॐ *Robert to Elizabeth,*

My own, now! For there it is!

❧28❧

My letters! all dead paper, . . mute and white! —
And yet they seem alive and quivering
Against my tremulous hands which loose the string
And let them drop down on my knee to-night.
This said, . . he wished to have me in his sight
Once, as a friend: this fixed a day in spring
To come and touch my hand . . . a simple thing,
Yet I wept for it! — this, . . the paper's light . .
Said, dear, I love thee; and I sank and quailed
As if God's future thundered on my past.
This said, I am thine — and so its ink has paled
With lying at my heart that beat too fast.
And this . . . O Love, thy words have ill availed,
If, what this said, I dared repeat at last!

𝕬 *Elizabeth to Robert*

But to say only that I was in the desert & that I am among the palm-trees, is to say nothing. . . because it is easy to *understand how*, after walking straight on . . on . . furlong after furlong . . dreary day after dreary day, . . one may come to the end of the sand & within sight of the fountain: – there is nothing miraculous in that, you know! –

𝕬 *Robert to Elizabeth*

Now bless you, my dearest, best Ba, for this letter which comes at the eleventh hour, – which means, at 3 o'clock: was not I fright-ened! [. . .] I was retreating as far as possible from that imaginary "woman who called out those feelings," – might have called them out, – just as this April sun of ours makes date-palms grow and bear – [. . .] you turn and ask "So your garden will rear palms"? Now, I tell Ba, . . no, I will kiss Ba and so tell her.

𝕬 *Elizabeth to Robert*

Ah – talking of palmtrees, you do not know what a curious coin-cidence your thought is with a thought of mine, which I shall not tell you now . . but some day perhaps.

29

I think of thee! — my thoughts do twine and bud
About thee, as wild vines, about a tree,
Put out broad leaves, and soon there's nought to see
Except the straggling green which hides the wood.
Yet, O my palm-tree, be it understood
I will not have my thoughts instead of thee
Who art dearer, better! rather instantly
Renew thy presence. As a strong tree should,
Rustle thy boughs and set thy trunk all bare,
And let these bands of greenery which insphere thee,
Drop heavily down, . . burst, shattered, everywhere!
Because, in this deep joy to see and hear thee
And breathe within thy shadow a new air,
I do not think of thee — I am too near thee.

᷐ *Elizabeth to Robert*

Only I know that if I went on to write disagreeing disagreeable letters [*she disagreed with Robert, who believed in dueling for honor*], you might not help to leave off loving me at the end. I seem to see through this crevice.

Good Heavens! – how dreadfully natural it would be to me, seem to me, if you DID leave off loving me! How it would be like the sun's setting . . & no more wonder! – Only, more darkness, more pain.

᷐ *Robert to Elizabeth*

Dearest, sweetest best – how can you, seeing so much, yet see that "possibility" – *I leave off loving* you! and be "angry" and "vexed" and the rest! [. . .] – it is a sense hitherto undreamed of, a new faculty – altogether an inexplicable, impossible feeling. [. . .] But I *can* fancy your being angry with me, very angry.

❧30❧

I see thine image through my tears tonight,
And yet to-day I saw thee smiling. How
Refer the cause? — Beloved, is it thou
Or I? who makes me sad? The acolyte
Amid the chanted joy and thankful rite,
May so fall flat, with pale insensate brow,
On the altar-stair. I hear thy voice and vow
Perplexed, uncertain, since thou art out of sight,
As he, in his swooning ears, the choir's amen.
Beloved, dost thou love? or did I see all
The glory as I dreamed, and fainted when
Too vehement light dilated my ideal,
For my soul's eyes? Will that light come again,
As now these tears come . . . falling hot and real?

❧ *Elizabeth to Robert*

It was just natural that when we differed for the first time I should fall into low spirits. In the night, at dream-time, [. . .] I have been sad even to tears [. . .] & whenever I am not *glad*, the old fears & misgivings come back — no, you *do not understand* . . you CANNOT, perhaps!

April 12, 1846

❧ *Robert to Elizabeth*

Dearest, — unspeakably dear Ba, [. . .] I feel I *must* live with you, — if but for a year, a month — to express the love which words cannot express, nor these letters, nor aught else.

31

Thou comest! all is said without a word.
I sit beneath thy looks, as children do
In the noon-sun, with souls that tremble through
Their happy eyelids from an unaverred
Yet prodigal inward joy. Behold, I erred
In that last doubt! and yet I cannot rue
The sin most, but the occasion . . . that we two
Should for a moment stand unministered
By a mutual presence. Ah, keep near and close,
Thou dovelike help! and, when my fears would rise,
With thy broad heart serenely interpose.
Brood down with thy divine sufficiencies
These thoughts which tremble when bereft of those,
Like callow birds left desert to the skies.

Written after their first meeting and Robert's profession of love:

❧ *Elizabeth to Robert*

I intended to write to you last night & this morning, & could not. [. . .] You have said some intemperate things . . . fancies, – which you will not say over again, nor unsay, but *forget at once, & for ever, having said at all,* – & which (so) will die out between *you & me alone,* like a misprint between you and the printer. [. . .] Now, if there should be one word of answer attempted to this, – or of reference; *I must not . . I* WILL *not see you again* & you will justify me later in your heart . . So for my sake you will not say it – I think you will not – & spare me the sadness of having to break through an intercourse just as it is promising pleasure to me, – to me who have so many sadnesses & so few pleasures. [. . .] I have much to receive from you in all the free gifts of thinking, teaching, master-spirits. [. . .] Your mistakes in me . . which *I* cannot mistake [. . .] I put away gently, & with grateful tears in my eyes.

July 1845

❧ *Robert to Elizabeth*

I shall just say, at the beginning of a note as at the end, I am yours *ever,* and not till summer ends & my nails fall out, and my breath breaks bubbles. [. . .] But with the soul, what is to be developed *afterward* is the main thing, and instinctively asserts its rights – so that when you hate (or love) you shall not be so able to explain "why." [. . .]

God bless you – do not be otherwise than kind to this letter which it costs me pains, great pains to avoid writing better, as truthfuller – this you get is not the first begun.

32

The first time that the sun rose on thine oath
To love me, I looked forward to the moon
To slacken all those bonds which seemed too soon
And quickly tied to make a lasting troth.
Quick-loving hearts, I thought, may quickly loathe;
And, looking on myself, I seemed not one
For such man's love! — more like an out of tune
Worn viol, a good singer would be wroth
To spoil his song with, and which, snatched in haste,
Is laid down at the first ill-sounding note.
I did not wrong myself so, but I placed
A wrong on thee. For perfect strains may float
'Neath master-hands, from instruments defaced, —
And great souls, at one stroke, may do and doat.

ও *Robert to Elizabeth*

Now I know it and write it – 'Ba' –and thank you. [. . .] So, wish by wish, one gets one's wishes! – at least I do – for one instance, you will go to Italy

ও *Robert to Elizabeth*

(But I have a new thing to say or sing – you never before heard me love and bless and send my heart after . . "Ba" – did you?) Ba . . and that is you! I TRIED . . (more than *wanted*) to call you *that*, on Wednesday! [. . .] You cannot tell how I feel glad that you will not part with the name – Barrett – seeing you have two of the same – and must always, moreover, remain my EBB!

❧33❧

Yes, call me by my pet-name! let me hear
The name I used to run at, when a child,
From innocent play, and leave the cowslips piled,
To glance up in some face that proved me dear
With the look of its eyes. I miss the clear
Fond voices, which, being drawn and reconciled
Into the music of Heaven's undefiled,
Call me no longer. Silence on the bier,
While I call God . . call God! — So let thy mouth
Be heir to those who are now exanimate.
Gather the north flowers to complete the south,
And catch the early love up in the late.
Yes, call me by that name, — and I, in truth,
With the same heart, will answer, and not wait.

From Elizabeth's "The Pet-Name" (1838), written two years before the death by drowning of her brother "Bro," who bestowed the pet-name "Ba" upon her:

> I have a name, a little name,
> Uncadenced for the ear,
> Unhonoured by ancestral claim,
> Unsanctified by prayer and psalm
> The solemn font anear. [. . .]
>
> My brother gave that name to me
> When we were children twain;
> When names acquired baptismally
> Were hard to utter, as to see
> That life had any pain. [. . .]
>
> Nay, do not smile! I hear in it
> What none of you can hear!
> The talk upon the willow seat,
> The bird and wind that did repeat
> Around, our human cheer.
>
> I hear the birthday's noisy bliss,
> My sisters' woodland glee,
> My father's praise I did not miss,
> When stooping down he cared to kiss
> The poet at his knee; – [. . .]
>
> My name to me a sadness wears;
> No murmurs cross my mind:
> Now God be thanked for these thick tears,
> Which show, of those departed years,
> Sweet memories left behind!

34

With the same heart, I said, I'll answer thee
As those, when thou shalt call me by my name —
Lo, the vain promise! is the same, the same,
Perplexed and ruffled by life's strategy?
When called before, I told how hastily
I dropped my flowers or brake off from a game,
To run and answer with the smile that came
At play last moment, and went on with me
Through my obedience. When I answer now,
I drop a grave thought, — break from solitude; —
Yet still my heart goes to thee . . . ponder how . .
Not as to a single good, but all my good!
Lay thy hand on it, best one, and allow
That no child's foot could run fast as this blood.

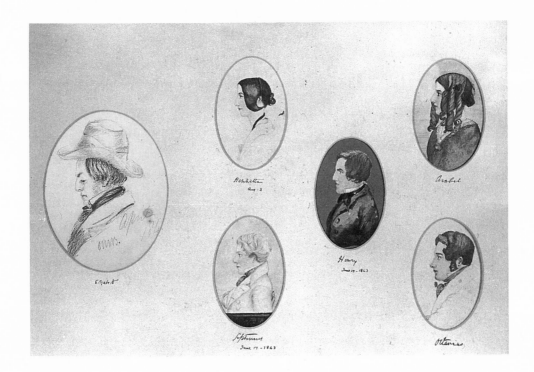

Portraits of Elizabeth's father, Edward Barrett Moulton Barrett (*left*), and her siblings Henrietta, Arabel, Henry, Septimus, and Octavius. The elder Moulton Barrett's portrait dates from 1847; the watercolors of the children, from 1843. All are by Elizabeth's brother Alfred.

🖤35🖤

If I leave all for thee, wilt thou exchange
And be all to me? Shall I never miss
Home-talk and blessing and the common kiss
That comes to each in turn, nor count it strange,
When I look up, to drop on a new range
Of walls and floors .. another home than this?
Nay, wilt thou fill that place by me which is
Filled by dead eyes too tender to know change?
That's hardest. If to conquer love, has tried,
To conquer grief, tries more . . . as all things prove;
For grief indeed is love and grief beside.
Alas, I have grieved so I am hard to love.
Yet love me — wilt thou? Open thine heart wide,
And fold within, the wet wings of thy dove.

ಇ∾ *Elizabeth to Robert*

Always I know, my beloved, that I am unworthy of your love in a hundred ways – yet I do hold fast my sense of advantage in one, – that, as far as I can see, I see after you . . understand you, divine you . . call you by your right name. Then it is something to be able to look at life itself as you look at it – (I quite *sigh* sometimes with satisfaction at that thought)! – there will be neither hope nor regret away from your footsteps. Dearest – I feel to myself sometimes, 'Do not move, do not speak – or the dream will vanish'! So fearfully like a dream, it is – Like a reflection in the water of an actual old, old dream of my own, too, . . touching which, . . now silent voices used to say "That romantic child"! –

❧36❧

When we met first and loved, I did not build
Upon the event with marble. Could it mean
To last, a love set pendulous between
Sorrow and sorrow? Nay, I rather thrilled,
Distrusting every light that seemed to gild
The onward path, and feared to overlean
A finger even. And, though I have grown serene
And strong since then, I think that God has willed
A still renewable fear . . O love, O troth . .
Lest these enclaspèd hands should never hold,
This mutual kiss drop down between us both
As an unowned thing, once the lips being cold.
And Love, be false! if he, to keep one oath,
Must lose one joy, by his life's star foretold.

ﻌ *Elizabeth to Robert*

I told you once that I never could love (in *this* way of love) except *upward* very far & high – but you are not like me in it, I thank God, – since you can love me. Love *me*, dearest of all – do not tire. I am your very own

Ba

ﻌ *Robert to Elizabeth*

Dearest Ba, I love you wholly and for ever – how shall the charm ever break?

My two letters! I think we must institute solemn days whereon such letters are to be read years hence . . when I shall ask you, – (all being known, many weaknesses you do not choose to see now, and perhaps some strength and constancy you cannot be sure of . . (for the charm may break, you think) . . "if you stood *there*" . . at Wimpole St. in the room . . would you whisper "Love, I love you, as before?"

37

Pardon, oh, pardon, that my soul should make
  Of all that strong divineness which I know
  For thine and thee, an image only so
Formed of the sand, and fit to shift and break.
  It is that distant years which did not take
  Thy sovranty, recoiling with a blow,
Have forced my swimming brain to undergo
  Their doubt and dread, and blindly to forsake
  Thy purity of likeness, and distort
Thy worthiest love to a worthless counterfeit.
  As if a shipwrecked Pagan, safe in port,
  His guardian sea-god to commemorate,
Should set a sculptured porpoise, gills a-snort,
  And vibrant tail, within the temple-gate.

ઌ *Robert to Elizabeth*

But to the end, the very end . . I am yours: God knows I would not do you harm for worlds – worlds! I may easily mistake what is harm or not. I will ask your leave to speak – at your foot, my Ba: I would not have dared to take the blessing of kissing your hand, much less your lip . . but that it seemed as if I was leading you into a mistake, – as did happen – and that you might fancy I only felt a dreamy, abstract passion for a phantom of my own creating out of your books and letters, and which only took your name. . . *That* once understood, the rest you shall give me. In every event, I am your own.

❧38❧

First time he kissed me, he but only kissed
The fingers of this hand wherewith I write;
And, ever since, it grew more clean and white, . .
Slow to world-greetings . . quick with its 'Oh, list,'
When the angels speak. A ring of amethyst
I could not wear here, plainer to my sight,
Than that first kiss. The second passed in height
The first, and sought the forehead, and half missed,
Half falling on the hair. O beyond meed!
That was the chrism of love, which love's own crown,
With sanctifying sweetness, did precede.
The third upon my lips was folded down
In perfect, purple state; since when, indeed,
I have been proud and said, 'My love, my own.'

ᘒ *Elizabeth to Robert*

I was out walking today again, & [. . .] I walked up all these stairs
with my own two feet on returning. I sate down on the stairs two or
three times, but I could not rest in the drawing-room because some-
body was there, & I was not carried, as usual – see how vainglorious
I am. And what a summer-sense in the air – & how lovely the strips
of sky between the houses! – And yet I may tell you truly [. . .] that
mournful and bitter would be to me this return into life, apart from
you, apart from the considerations of you. How could ever I have
borne it, I keep feeling constantly. But you are there, in the place of
memory.

❧39❧

Because thou hast the power and own'st the grace
To look through and behind this mask of me,
(Against which years have beat thus blanchingly
With their rains,) and behold my soul's true face,
The dim and weary witness of life's race! —
Because thou has the faith and love to see,
Through that same soul's distracting lethargy,
The patient angel waiting for a place
In the new Heavens! — because nor sin nor woe,
Nor God's infliction, nor death's neighbourhood,
Nor all which others viewing, turn to go, . .
Nor all which makes me tired of all, self-viewed, . .
Nothing repels thee, . . Dearest, teach me so
To pour out gratitude, as thou dost, good.

December 21, 1845

ॐ *Elizabeth to Robert*

People used to say to me, "You expect too much – you are too ro-
mantic – " And my answer always was that "I could not expect too
much when I expected nothing at all" .. which was the truth – for I
never thought (& how often I have SAID *that!*) I never thought that
anyone whom *I* could love, would stoop to love ME .. the two things
seemed clearly incompatible to my understanding. [. . .]

It is true of me .. very true .. that I have not a high appreciation of
what passes in the world [. . .] under the name of love; & that a dis-
trust of the thing had grown to be a habit of mind with me when I
knew you first. It has appeared to me, through all the seclusion of
my life & the narrow experience it admitted of, that in nothing,
men .. & women too! .. were so apt to mistake their own feelings, as
in this one thing. [. . .] To see the marriages which are made every
day! – worse than solitudes & more desolate! In the case of the two
happiest I ever knew, one of the husbands said in confidence to a
brother of mine – not much in confidence or I should not have
heard it, but in a sort of smoking frankness .. that he had "ruined his
prospects by marrying"; & the other said to himself at the very mo-
ment of profession an extraordinary happiness, . . "But I should
have done as well if I had not married *her*."

August 12, 1846

ॐ *Elizabeth to Robert*

When women are chosen for wives, they are not chosen for com-
panions. [. . .] Men like to come home & find a blazing fire & a smil-
ing face & an hour of relaxation. Their serious thoughts [. . .] they
like to keep to one side. And this is the carrying out of love & mar-
riage almost everywhere in the world – & this, the degrading of
women by both.

40

Oh, yes! they love through all this world of ours!
I will not gainsay love, called love forsooth.
I have heard love talked in my early youth,
And since, not so long back but that the flowers
Then gathered, smell still. Mussulmans and Giaours
Throw kerchiefs at a smile, and have no ruth
For any weeping. Polypheme's white tooth
Slips on the nut, if, after frequent showers,
The shell is over-smooth, — and not so much
Will turn the thing called love, aside to hate,
Or else to oblivion. But thou art not such
A lover, my Beloved! thou canst wait
Through sorrow and sickness, to bring souls to touch,
And think it soon when others cry 'Too late.'

&ear; *Elizabeth to Robert*

O my angel at the gate of the prison!

Elizabeth Barrett, with her dog Flush, at 50 Wimpole Street. The sketch, by her brother Alfred, is dated December 12, 1843.

An engraved portrait of Robert Browning that hung on Elizabeth's bedroom wall before she met the poet.

❧41❧

I thank all who have loved me in their hearts,
With thanks and love from mine. Deep thanks to all
Who paused a little near the prison-wall,
To hear my music in its louder parts,
Ere they went onward, each one to the mart's
Or temple's occupation, beyond call.
But thou, who, in my voice's sink and fall,
When the sob took it, thy divinest Art's
Own instrument didst drop down at thy foot,
To harken what I said between my tears, . .
Instruct me how to thank thee! — Oh, to shoot
My soul's full meaning into future years,
That they should lend it utterance, and salute
Love that endures, from Life that disappears!

My future will not copy fair my past
On any leaf but Heaven's. Be fully done,
Supernal Will! I would not fain be one
Who, satisfying thirst and breaking fast
Upon the fulness of the heart, at last
Says no grace after meat. My wine hath run
Indeed out of my cup, and there is none
To gather up the bread of my repast
Scattered and trampled; – yet I find some good
In earth's green herbs, and streams that bubble up
Clear from the darkling ground, – content until
I sit with angels before better food.
Dear Christ! when Thy new vintage fills my cup,
This hand shall shake no more, nor that wine spill.

November 16, 1845

Robert to Elizabeth

And since I wrote what is above, I have been reading among other poems that sonnet – "Past and Future" – which affects me more than any poem I ever read.

November 17, 1845

Elizabeth to Robert

I never have doubted you. [. . .] I thought [. . .] that you were self-deceived as to the nature of your own feelings. [. . .] I had been shut up here too long face to face with my own spirit, not to know myself, &, so, to have lost the common illusions of vanity. All the men I had ever known could not make your stature among them. So it was not distrust, but reverence rather. I sate by while the angel stirred the water, & I called it Messiah. Do not blame me now, . . *my* angel!

42

'My future will not copy fair my past' —
I wrote that once; and thinking at my side
My ministering life-angel justified
The word by his appealing look upcast
To the white throne of God, I turned at last,
And there, instead, saw thee, not unallied
To angels in thy soul! Then I, long tried
By natural ills, received the comfort fast,
While budding, at thy sight, my pilgrim's staff
Gave out green leaves with morning dews impearled.
I seek no copy now of life's first half:
Leave here the pages with long musing curled,
And write me new my future's epigraph,
New angel mine, unhoped for in the world!

᷂ *Robert to Elizabeth*

Yesterday morning as I turned to look for a book, an old fancy seized me to try the "sortes" and dip into the first page of the first I chanced upon, for my fortune; I said "what will be the event of my love for Her" – in so many words – and my book turned out to be – "Cerutti's Italian Grammar" – a propitious source of information . . the best to be hoped, what could it prove but some assurance that you were in the Dative Case, or I, not in the ablative absolute? [. . .] Well, I ventured – and what did I find? *This* – which I copy from the book now – *"If we love in the other world as we do in this, I shall love thee to eternity"* – from "Promiscuous Exercises," to be translated into Italian, at the end.

February 12, 1846

᷂ *Elizabeth to Robert*

Ah, the 'sortes'! – It is a double oracle [. . .] – "I shall love thee to eternity" – I *shall.*

43

How do I love thee? Let me count the ways.
I love thee to the depth and breadth and height
My soul can reach, when feeling out of sight
For the ends of Being and ideal Grace.
I love thee to the level of everyday's
Most quiet need, by sun and candlelight.
I love thee freely, as men strive for Right;
I love thee purely, as they turn from Praise.
I love thee with the passion put to use
In my old griefs, and with my childhood's faith.
I love thee with a love I seemed to lose
With my lost saints, — I love thee with the breath,
Smiles, tears, of all my life! — and, if God choose,
I shall but love thee better after death.

❧ *Elizabeth to Robert*

Count among the miracles that your flowers live with me – I accept that for an omen, dear – dearest! Flowers in general, all other flowers, die of despair when they come into the same atmosphere . . used to do it so constantly & observably that it made me melancholy & I left off for the most part having them here. Now, you see how they put up with the close room, & condescend to me & the dust – it is true and no fancy! To be sure they know that I care for them & that I stand up by the table myself to change their water & cut their stalks freshly at intervals – that may make the difference perhaps. Only the great reason must be that they are yours, & that you teach them to bear with me patiently.

July 19, 1846

❧ *Robert to Elizabeth*

I wish, dearest, you would tell me precisely what you have written – all my affectionate pride in you rises at once when I think of your poetry, that is and that is to be – you dear, dear Ba, can you not write on my shoulder while my head lies as you permit?

July 22, 1846

❧ *Elizabeth to Robert*

You shall see some day at Pisa what I will not show you now. Does not Solomon say that 'there is a time to read what is written.' If he doesn't, he *ought*.

❧ *Note by Elizabeth at the bottom of the British Library manuscript of the final sonnet:*

50 Wimpole Street
1846, Sept.
Married – September 12th,
1846.

❧44❧

Beloved, thou hast brought me many flowers
Plucked in the garden, all the summer through
And winter, and it seemed as if they grew
In this close room, nor missed the sun and showers.
So, in the like name of that love of ours,
Take back these thoughts which here unfolded too,
And which on warm and cold days I withdrew
From my heart's ground. Indeed, those beds and bowers
Be overgrown with bitter weeds and rue,
And wait thy weeding; yet here's eglantine,
Here's ivy!—take them, as I used to do
Thy flowers, and keep them where they shall not pine.
Instruct thine eyes to keep their colours true,
And tell thy soul, their roots are left in mine.

"View from drawingroom in Casa Valeri, Bagni Caldi, Bagni di Lucca," a sketch by Elizabeth Barrett Browning.

Elizabeth did not show the sonnets to Robert during their honeymoon in Pisa as she had promised. It was three years later, after the birth of their son Pen, on holiday in Lucca, that she handed them to Robert. "When Robert saw them he was much touched & pleased – & thinking highly of the poetry he did not let, could not consent, he said, that they should be lost to my volumes." The previously unpublished drawing above was sent to her sister Arabel from Lucca on July 4, 1849, and records the view Robert would remember sixteen years later.

ɞ *Robert to Julia Wedgwood*

 Yes, that was a strange, heavy crown, that wreath of Sonnets, put
on me one morning, unawares, three years after it had been twined,
– all this delay, because I happened early to say something against
putting one's loves into verse: then again, I said something else on
the other side, one evening at Lucca, – and next morning she said
hesitatingly "Do you know I once wrote some poems about *you?*" –
and then – "There they are, if you care to see them," and there was
the little Book I have here – with the last Sonnet dated two days be-
fore our marriage. How I see the gesture, and hear the tones, – and,
for the matter of that, see the window at which I was standing, with
the tall mimosa in front, and little church-court to the right. After-
ward the publishing them was through me – in the interest of the
poet, I chose that they should be added to the other works, not
minding the undue glory to me, if the fact should become transpar-
ent: there was a trial at covering it a little by leaving out one sonnet
[Sonnet 42] which had plainly a connexion with her former works:
but it was put in afterwards when people chose to pull down the
mask which, in old days, people used to respect at a masquerade.
But I never cared. "The Portuguese" – purposely an ambiguous title
– was that Caterina who left Camoens the riband from her hair.

ๆ *Robert to Elizabeth*

You speak out, *you,* – I only make men & women speak.

ๆ *Robert to Elizabeth (on the eve of their departure to Italy)*

Write to me one word more – depend on me.

Your own, own R.

ๆ *Elizabeth to Robert (her one word more)*

Your letters to me I take with me, let the 'ounces' cry out aloud ever so. I *tried* to leave them, & I could not. That is, they would not be left: it was not my fault – I will not be scolded.

Is this my last letter to you, ever dearest? [. . .]

Do you pray for me tonight, Robert? Pray for me, & love me, that I may have courage, feeling both –

Your own Ba –

The boxes are *safely* sent. Wilson [her maid] has been perfect to me – And *I* . . calling her "timid," & afraid of her timidity! – I begin to think that none are so bold as the timid, when they are fairly roused.

ONE WORD MORE: TO E.B.B.

What were seen? None knows, none ever shall know.
Only this is sure — the sight were other,
Not the moon's same side, born late in Florence,
Dying now impoverished here in London.
God be thanked, the meanest of his creatures
Boasts two soul-sides, one to face the world with,
One to show a woman when he loves her!

This I say of me, but think of you, Love!
This to you — yourself my moon of poets!
Ah, but that's the world's side, there's the wonder,
Thus they see you, praise you, think they know you!
There, in turn I stand with them and praise you —
Out of my own self, I dare to phrase it.
But the best is when I glide from out them,
Cross a step or two of dubious twilight,
Come out on the other side, the novel
Silent silver lights and darks undreamed of,
Where I hush and bless myself with silence.